Long Reach Home

Dianne Hicks Morrow

2

Long Reach Home

Dianne Hicks Morrow

The Acorn Press
Charlottetown
Prince Edward Island
2002

Long Reach Home
ISBN 1-894838-00-9

Cover image: *Pam's Place* by Sylvia Ridgway, from a Private Collection
Cover photography: John Sylvester
Editing: Jane Ledwell
Design: Matthew MacKay
Printing: Williams & Crue (1982) Ltd., Summerside, PEI

The Acorn Press gratefully acknowledges the support of
The Canada Council for the Arts.

National Library of Canada Cataloguing in Publication Data

Morrow, Dianne Hicks, 1946–
    Long reach home

Poems.
ISBN 1-894838-00-9
    I. Title.
PS8576.O744L66 2002   C811'.6   C2002-901105-1
PR9199.4.M658L66 2002

The Acorn Press
P.O. Box 22024
Charlottetown,
Prince Edward Island
Canada C1A 9J2

www.acornpresscanada.com

7 sections
sepia-like
white picket fence
drawing at the
opening of each
chapter (divider)

For my mother
Mary Daw Hicks
who still teaches me how to see

In memory of my father
Lorne Bentley Hicks
who taught me
the pleasure of a walk in the woods
the joy of rowing a boat
and that girls should have strong biceps

I honour your lives and your relationship.

published by
grant from
PEI Council of the
Arts

lack of metaphor,
heavily narrative,
descriptive /
lacks interpretive
qualities in
spite of its
nuances of
emotion and
intelligence

Contents

Long Reach

Scripting Love

Motherlode

Motherlode 2

Familiars

Polio Kick

Home

Long Reach

St. John River Suite

1. 8 A.M. FLIGHT

Bits of land float
on a wide river through green
splashed blue by lakes and ponds,
puzzle pieces
thirty-five thousand feet below.

Suddenly they start to make sense—
Spoon Island, The Mistake, Grassy Island,
Oak Point, Brown's Flat, Caton's Island.
My body buzzes with memories:
the camp built on stilts on Victoria Beach,
my father priming the pump,
the best drinking water anywhere,
fireflies twinkling along the track to the rock cut,
the view from the trestle over my valley of Eden
where I paddled with my first boyfriend.

Morning suns The Devil's Back on Long Reach.

Kid-like, I lean
across the tiny window,
search out every landmark.
Can't quite make out the seven camps,
only the fingernail of beach against dark trees.
Too bad if the stranger in the aisle seat
wants to see anything. I hear him ask,
"You from Ottawa?"

Below me the only place
where I still know
how to do nothing.

I fill my eyes to the brim
until the wing swallows for me.
I look at the stranger and answer,
"No, I'm from down there."

2. LEAF RAKER

Ape-like, his hairy arms grasp
the tree branch above his head.
His feet bounce up and down
inside a jumbo Glad bag,
tamping down,
whooshing air out
from a zillion leaves:
my eighty-year-old father
with a weak heart, determined
to fit in every last leaf.

3. REACHER

On Long Reach he leans the rotting ladder—
angled too steep for safety—
against the front of the camp on high stilts.
I see the rock in the soft sand behind him,
the spot his head would hit.

anticipation
of dread

"For God's sake, Dad, leave
the spider web up there.
Who cares?"

He does.
But he puts the ladder down.

Dianne Hicks Morrow

4. FIXER-UPPER

His lined face glows as
he roots in the wall cabinet,
each tiny box a memory:
brass screws left over
from his wood projects,
glazier points from plate glass windows.
But there's no tape to stop
the air leak in his old water pump,
still here nine years after
he sold the camp.
Now the pump spouts
as much air as water.

This won't do.
The pump is the heart.

12

Granny Beat

Beatrice Fanny was wise
despite frivolous airs:

> Now me maids wha's 'is name?
> My tha's a fine lookin' fella.
> Where's she off to all dressed up like a crit?
> Got 'er cap set for 'im I'd say.
> Let's 'ave a 'and a cards.

At twelve I learned to be the fourth
at Bridge when newly widowed Beat
came to stay a few months.
The first time I held thirteen cards
all thumbs and so many rules
I had nightmares
about the Queen of Hearts:
off with her head, off with her head.

Granny shared my room each winter
until I went away to college.
I got used to her snores and
teeth in a glass by the bed.
How vexed she got the night
I slipped dulse under her pillow
for a joke.

> How can you eat that stinky seaweed?

Late some nights I'd ask,
"Tell me about when you were young."

> Ah my dear, there's not much to tell
> I did go up to Canada when I was eighteen.
> Got to go 'cause stodgy E. J. Pratt, the poet,
> promised my folks he'd keep an eye on me.
> Not an ounce of fun in that man,

hard to believe he's a Newfoundlander.
Long boat ride, long train ride.
I hardly ever saw him after that.
Got a job in Toronto at Eaton's,
the ladies department,
grand clothes, all the modern styles.
I was a proper crit.
The great Watt Spracklan often asked me to skate.

"Granny did you fall in love?"

Yes my dear, now and then, but you know
I came home and married your grandfather.
My, how I miss him.

*   *   *

Grampy Jack, soft-spoken man,
read to me in bed when I was seven.
His brown eyes glistened
at a sad part of *The Water Babies*,
my mother's favourite story when
she was little. I knew then
why she loved him so.
"Grampy, I hope you die last."

Wet-eyed he whispered,
        You mustn't ever say that.

Then a slight smile and,
        Thank you dear,

so I knew it was okay.

But he died first anyway.

Christmas Eve

Eight-year-old doubting Thomasina,
I ask my mother, "How will Santa find me
on the train?" Miles and miles of
Christmasy trees speed by the window
as she covers me up and explains,
"He knows where you are, you'll see."
I want to believe.
Visions of my dream dolly
dance through my head, then fade.
How will he even get on this train
and will he know I'm the girl who
wants the large-as-life doll?
I drift in and out of fitful sleep,
want to be awake to tell him,
I'd be in my own bed at home 'cept we're going
to Montreal for Christmas with my cousins.
No sign of Santa—where is he? *Is he?*

One eye opens to daylight and motion.
Where am I? Mom and Dad asleep across from me,
baby asleep beside me—What baby?
"He came, he came!" I yell. *He is, he is.*
 Mom and Dad are happy to tell me,
"He got on the train in Sherbrooke, Quebec."
I believe, I believe, I believe he did.
Here is Chuckles, so lifelike
the conductor has to do a recount,
one extra head on this train
since crossing the border. A stowaway?
I'm thrilled when he asks if this is
my baby sister or a doll.

Chuckles' big blue eyes open and close,
real lashes, not painted on.
Dimpled elbows and knees, flushed baby cheeks,
her body soft in her hand-knitted dress.

Dianne Hicks Morrow

Only the raised rubber curls give her away,
if you look under her knitted bonnet.

My Santa-on-the-train story leaves
doubting older cousins speechless.

Back home one winter night
Mom and Dad have friends in for Bridge.
Awake in bed I overhear them talk.
"How did you get that big doll on the train?"
"I'll tell you it wasn't easy. It took
up most of the space in one suitcase!"
In the dark I blush, don't let on
I hear, even to myself.

would have been a good to place start

Pane by Pane

Our boots tromp
storm windows
lying on the autumn lawn.
Giggling, we feel glass
crunch underfoot.
My best friend and I know
we are bad, but
can't stop laughing,
can't stop stomping—
pane by pane—
until all are shiny shards.

Later Dad says,
"I can't imagine what hooligans
would smash Paul's windows.
You wouldn't know anything
about this, would you?"
I lie.
Forty-five years later
I confess.
Dad shakes
his head and says, "Stupid
place for Paul to leave
those windows, wasn't it?"

forgiveness in perspective

17

Dianne Hicks Morrow

I Learned How

I learned how to row Dad's duck boat
biceps bulging in my toothpick arms,
mesmerized by the swirling 0 and number 7
each oar made coming out of the water.

One lazy day, Elaine and I
rowed downriver,
fed mints to a sleek puppy
who followed the boat back home,
his rounded head and snout so sweet
as he took each candy from my hand,
until I saw his feet were webbed
and screamed. Elaine rowed for our lives.
The thing followed, belly
dragging on the shore as we landed.
The nearest neighbour jumped in his dory.
"Gotta chase it out. Gotta find its mother."
Seeing our shocked faces, he added,
"They ruin our nets, girls. Sea lions.
You're lucky not to lose your fingers."

Once we rowed far out
for safe skinny-dipping—the river
of my childhood a mile wide.
We slipped off swimsuits underwater,
felt freshwater silk all over,
the thrill of climbing back in the boat
to dive naked. We blushed
when the neighbours told on us.
We'd not gone out far enough.

Looking Down

We scrabble up,
twist ankles in rock slides
of our own making.
Panting, we sit on the edge
in the shade of spindly trees,
look down at the river sparkle,
our parents bright pebbles on the beach.
Along the sandy shore
seven rooftops,
postage stamps on a letter
from far away, in a language
we suddenly understand.
Drunk with omniscience, we
make wise pronouncements, know
that we'll remember this as long as we live.

At school Monday we'll
pretend we don't know each other,
me, a girl three grades ahead;
you, the handsome boy who
towers over me.

no interior narrative

Dianne Hicks Morrow

Suddenly the Dusky Sky

Pubescent we straggle
along railway tracks to the rockcut
where three men died, dynamite blast
a century ago. We spook ourselves,
look down at jagged boulders,
see blood and bone.

Suddenly the dusky sky
splashes orange, pink, purple,
then charcoal grey, right over our heads.
Air crackles, hairs stand on end.
We make ourselves dizzy
leaping from tie to tie, looking
up to make sure it's still there
swirling above us.
The sky is falling.
This is the end of the world.

What is it about? disparate themes

Scripting Love

All the Right Things

Dazzled by her exuberance
he asked her home from the dance.
Nearly there she said let's stop,
led him down a steep path
to a bluff over the ocean.
Awed by the canopy of stars,
moonbeam on satin sea,
they touched shyly
in keeping with the calm.

She wore his adoration like an old jacket.
Kept her warm while she looked for a
new one, smarter with more style.
He took her to meet his parents,
held her hand all the way to the airport,
teary-eyed flew to college far away.
He wrote every week, surprised
her with the poetry of his words.

Months later she heard his Harley
below her apartment late one night,
home from college, homesick for her.
She asked him in to meet her friend,
brooding campus radical who read
all the right things, veiled his feelings
in arts major lingo, feared the
openness of this competitor.

The Harley roared away.
She went all the way that night
to prove she had made the right choice.

Seaside Park

"Remember the Partridge Island light?
Eight seconds between flashes.
We counted them with swigs of rum."
Did I learn to like rum with him?
I know I liked his gentlemanly
touch, Lebanon in his eyes.
I don't remember
being here with him.

Our brown eyes lock
three decades after summer jobs
at the World Famous
Reversing Falls Restaurant
and Tourist Bureau.

A set of sturdy stairs
climbs the cliff from the beach,
top landing covers the grassy place
where we counted falling stars.
That silvery night floats back, now.
The light flashes every eight seconds.

*what connection
does he make ?
involve him ~
create some
fiction
around
it*

23

Dianne Hicks Morrow

In my dream you

are downriver
at someone else's camp.
Four of us sit around
a fish tank of exotics,
one spotted gold and silver.
Your deep brown eyes
speckled gold
look exotic to me,
your sudden smile punctuates
the hint of Yankee accent
still there after all these years.
One woman grows summer savoury.
I want to buy some,
savour summers past.
We eat thick steaks of halibut
cooked by the other woman who
has found extra for me.
The looks you give
me are as delicious
as the flakes of fish.

24

who are these woman?

A sudden sap runs

[handwritten annotation: lovely title]

in my forty-six-year-old trunk.
I am twenty-one in hot Amsterdam,
entranced by a California boy's
book choices and bronzed body.
Both of us are reading *The Great Gatsby*,
both have loved Robert Frost,
both have lovers back home.
Four magic days.

Today, it's an April Fools' Day snowstorm.
We begin with a passionate argument.
Four hours later we end
with a passionate gaze.
Your hand strokes my cheek.
I pull away, settle for safety.
We know what has happened
will hold us.

[handwritten annotation: confusion of upper and lower case titles lettering]

Middle-Aged Women Who Flirt

Haven't thought about men
in years, except the three
I live with: husband and two sons.

But now I have three
crushes on the go.
How can this be?

At a meeting Julie says,
"You look like you're in love.
Which sex?"

Eliza Jane says it's hormones.

At quilting Anne says mid-life
women often have flirtations
just before they lose
their looks for good.

Owl Woman

You call me owl woman
in my new reading glasses.
Wish I were, wise I mean,
like my father, who
tells a story for each
picture in the owl calendar
his grandson gives him
on his eighty-third birthday.
An hour passes and the stories do not.
His grandson fidgets.

Does he recall hooting at owls?
Late one night you took us
to hear their mating calls,
his baby eyes wide
as he mimicked the sounds.

I remember the whoosh
of owl wings on a marsh walk
with you before our son was born.
Now he wings to college
near that marsh.

A shock of sudden movement
startles me from my driver's trance—
through the windshield,
white underwings, luminescent.
An owl that close must mean something.

domestic encounters gives voice to unspoken intergenerational dialogues

beautifully designed volume

27

Dianne Hicks Morrow

You need to know

I'd rather be content
cross-country skiing
than ecstatic
downhilling
because after the ecstasy
comes the long cold
line-up for the lift.

I like to lift myself,
feel the strain of muscle
until my body relaxes
into the rhythm,
stroke and glide, stroke and glide.
The groomed trail guides me
to quiet delights.

My skis stroke smooth slopes,
glide on silken snow
undulating beneath me.

28

Motherlode

We Enter the House of Her Childhood

We enter the house of her childhood
when her eyes still worked.
She tells me how it was—
carved hall tree in the foyer,
bevelled glass French doors her crowd
waltzed through into the diningroom.
The hardwood floors still glow. Mom's dainty
fingers trace the diamond-shaped panes
in the door to the breakfast room.

The lonely widower living here now
proudly tells us the bell system still works.
Six buzzers make six arrows point
to show the maid in the kitchen
which room rang. When Mom asks,
"Do the fish still point upward?"
I just say yes.
They are arrows, not fish.
The backstairs are gone from the maid's room
to the pantry, where my mother and her sister
sneaked late-night treats.
The pantry is a woodshed.

In the huge bedroom Mom shared with Aunt Joan,
the marble fireplace is blocked.
My eyes zoom in on the triple window,
cut out the gaudy 70s wallpaper to
picture unchanged panes where
Mom looked over Bay Roberts Harbour
and her father's general store. Miss Mary
and Miss Joan hoping for penny candy,
listening to old men yarn, watching
the fishing boats come in. Now
a rink-sized concrete slab shows
where the store was;
not a hint of the wharf behind it.

I tell her this is one time when it is better to be blind.

beautifully
embellished
description but
no requirement
for interpretation

31

finely nuanced
and delicately
sensitive
emotional
motifs

Dianne Hicks Morrow

Newfoundland War Bride

Your married sister comes home for the engagement party,
surprised it's not your law-school-bound longtime boyfriend,
but a well-mannered sailor
from a New Brunswick farm,
still a bachelor at thirty-one.

Nine years younger, what are you thinking?
A merchant's daughter, sea captain's granddaughter,
marrying a Canadian who plans to take you back
to a Northern Ontario gold mine
once this war is over.
You know you'll never be a lawyer,
now you can't read the fine print.

You cup your ear to the panelled mahogany doors,
hear Lorne clear his throat and ask
for your hand in marriage,
strain to hear your father say,
"Mary may lose her sight."
Lorne's voice is clear:
"Then I'll do the seeing for both of us."

White Cane

Four years old. I tiptoe across the room,
wave at the woman on the phone.
Her eyes don't follow me.
How can she tell
if my hand's in the candy dish,
if I'm drawing on walls,
if I'm silently sad?
Is my mother blind?

Grade one. I run home after school.
Door locked, wine-coloured curtains closed.
I knock. Mom lets me in,
introduces an older woman I've
never seen before. She
has piercing eyes,
grills me like school.
She teaches my mother to
read Braille and touch type
in three days, a record.
Mom refuses to learn the white cane.

Grade seven. Mom's on the phone
to tell my teacher:
"Just want you to know I'll be in hospital.
Oh, cataracts.
A bit of trouble threading needles."
Threading needles? She can't
see the cloth. Can't see me.
No one guesses what
it takes for her to keep
frayed edges
from unravelling.

her mother's blindness —

first person missing

enters others' experience by means of her own

33

Dianne Hicks Morrow

Guide Rope

The thing you liked best about the camp was
going down the steps onto soft sand,
reaching for the hand-high
white rope Dad put on stakes
for you to follow to the water.
You'd spread his Navy-issue canvas
on the beach, turn the heavy transistor
radio on high, tie it to the end
of the rope and walk alone
into the wide river. You'd swim back
and forth along the shore, tethered to a lifeline
of staccato announcements and fading AM music.

34

Piano Lessons

1. WHAT DID YOU THINK WHEN

you heard me pounding
middle C so hard
the ivory broke?
A rotten front tooth
on the second-hand
walnut upright,
its curly cutouts
backed by faded damask.
Did you wonder why you'd
made Dad spend scarce dollars
to have this piano crowd
your tiny diningroom?
You loved to play the piano as a child.
You can't play this one at all.
Can no longer see the notes,
can't play without them.

2. MUSIC FESTIVAL

Stiff turquoise organdy dress,
raised pink polka dots.
Sweaty hands folded
in my lap, head down.
My mother's words in my ears,
"Don't play it too fast, dear."

Try to tune out the high-pitched
chatter of the girl beside me.
"I just know I'm gonna make a mistake,
don't you? Aren't you nervous? How much longer?"

She will play last, right after me.
Thirty others fidget through

the ten-and-under line-up.
All play so fast they make mistakes.

"Feel my hands. They're
shaking. Aren't yours?"
Not yet, but if you don't shut up.
My turn.
Knees knock across the endless stage,
hands adjust the bench,
feet find the pedals.

Begin to play.
Not like them.
Nice and slow.
Never
played
it
this
slow
before.
No wrong notes.
The final bar.

36

I see my mother's face in the audience.
She's not smiling. Later she asks,
"Dear, why did you play it like a dirge?"

3. STOP

"I think it's time to stop
your piano lessons. You won't practise.
It's a waste of a dollar a week."

"Aw Mom, I can't quit.
How will the nuns know anything
about the world if I don't tell them?"
I'd introduced them
to Broadway musicals.
When I refused to do any more theory
my mother let me buy sheet music.
The convent piano had never played
"I'm Gonna Wash that Man Right Outta My Hair."

My teacher couldn't get the rhythm
of "Surrey with a Fringe on Top"
until I hummed it for her.
Showed me that if you hadn't
heard a song before
you couldn't get it right
even if you were a piano teacher
and a nun.

intelligent child

4. LET ME HEAR

"What long piano fingers.
Let me hear you play, dear."
The nun tries to hide her disappointment
when I look up after the last chord
but agrees to take me on.
I wonder if there's any hair
under her wimple; decide after a few
lessons I want to be a nun.
Mom looks stunned. I spell it out.
"A n-o-n-e!"

Dianne Hicks Morrow

I didn't know she'd tried
to stop her best friend
from taking final vows,
sneaked into the convent
the night before to try again.
Forty years later I meet an aged nun
in a swimming pool, on holiday,
tell her my mother's best friend became a nun.
"I can't think of her name, but she taught music."
"Sister Mary Katherine? She's up there in cabin 8.
Doesn't like to swim, allergic to the sun.
I'll tell her you're here."

Seated, back straight, she's my
mother's opposite, tall and thin,
face pale as her long-sleeved blouse.
Only her voice shows excitement.
"Maim's daughter. Last time I saw your mother
we were eighteen. What fun
we had growing up in Bay Roberts.
Just imagine, your staying at these cabins too.
Tell me all about Maim."

unclosed narrative

Back home I tell Mom the story.
Soon they are sending tapes back and forth.
Mom hears the music in her voice,
"Christmas cards come
from all over the world, people
I taught as children."

Mom's dainty hands
and light touch
make the piano sing
when she plays
the only tune
she remembers.

Glamour

Gaggle of girls in residence perform
nightly beauty rituals, preen for morning parade.
Rollers wrench scalp and sleep.
What man would ever want to see us this way?
Have long years of swinging hair, luscious lips,
and Cleopatra eyes enslaved us to *Glamour*?

I slam the magazine on the floor.
But the button-down cover girl's
tiny nose and perfect smile
still face me.

I throw out my makeup.
Some voice in me still tut-tuts.
So does my mother who hasn't seen
me since blurred babyhood.
"Your Aunt Joan says it's a shame
you stopped wearing makeup."
Mom freshens her lipstick
every few hours.

Dianne Hicks Morrow

The Blind Driver

Behind the wheel,
she trusts me to guide her
through the traffic.

Turn a little left, oops, I mean right
no, not that far
come back this way—
phew, we just missed that car—
oh God, the brick wall.

I wake screaming
over and over.

Tonight the blind singer
tells how he learned to drive.
Words don't work
for him either
but someone's hands
on his shoulders
from the seat
behind him do.

Their touch angles him
the same degree
as the wheel
needs to turn
to keep the car
on the road.

My mother doesn't
want to drive.
Why must I dream
she does,
that my job is to
outsmart brick walls?

Dianne Hicks Morrow

Dream: Deserted

Adobe building, desert out the window,
stone steps worn down by passing
feet. Water flows up the stairs as fast
as I can climb them. There are three storeys,
so I'm not worried. But now I have my mother
to guide. We never like our heads
under water. As we reach the top
of the stairs I know we will drown.

*   *   *

At a bazaar I'm waiting for a rickety bus
weaving too fast among crowds of colour—
people, donkeys, hens and dogs.
The bus stops. My father is driving. I can't
hide my surprise to see him. He says
he's looking for my mother. He last saw
her in a bazaar at the next oasis.

*   *   *

42

I'm inside thick-walled adobe looking
into harsh sunlight. The doorway arch frames
the hubbub of the narrow street. Through the crowd
I see my mother groping
along a rough wall until the alleyway
stops her. Her arm reaches
to find a new wall to follow.
She does not look afraid. I should run
to help her, but I just keep watching.

Motherlode 2

Push Mower

Cocooning me
in white noise
my mower unwinds
my thoughts:
ideas sprout,
grow, flower.
My children mouth silent o's
in their sandbox every spin
round the house. I wave
and mow on.
Two hours of sweat
for a green paradise.
First thing
since motherhood
to stay done
a few days.

images:
few metaphors
of
complexity

44

* Power Failure   *excellent*

Wired for
reception,
I am charged
with the current
of anyone's pain,
pick up
sorrow,
anger,
fear.
Powerless
to shut down,
my circuits blow.

Dianne Hicks Morrow

Dispenser

I am not in-
dispensable,
dispense with me,
please. I am
not your life-
line, dis-
connect me
now.
I am not in. - *last lines weaken impact*

46

Do It Yourself

No wonder I feel like a failure—
in this culture mothers must
meet others' needs before their own
or face the silent stares
of those they love
and the judgement of experts
who write how-to essays:

hand-sew Halloween costumes
for your pre-schoolers while
taking West Coast conference calls
on your speaker phone in the comfort
of your home office, its fire-
place glowing with hardwood
you've chopped weekends
from your hundred-acre
woodlot to keep your cholesterol down.

Hell, all I want is a guilt-
free hour to write some poetry.

47

Dianne Hicks Morrow

Double Message

Hi Boys,
There are four hotdogs thawed in the fridge.
The buns are in the warming oven.
Have some yogurt
and bananas.

The scrap of paper
is full.
No space for
Love, Mom.
Leaves me thinking
about other things not said:

Four hugs warm in my arms
when I come back from work.
The buns have messages in them:
You will lead a charmed life.
No accident will befall you.
Joy and contentment will be yours.
You will not try to save face
at any cost.
You will understand women
as well as men.

But I'd settle for:
Don't skate on the pond.
Don't slide down the icy hill.
Don't forget to turn off the stove
after you cook the hotdogs.
Don't forget to be kind to each other
forever.
Love, Mom.

48

Instinct

I needn't have worried. Our
teenaged mother cat knows
how to raise her kittens,
and has a thing or two to teach
me about setting boundaries
and letting go.

Sleek mama cat crosses kitchen floor,
scowls at son nearly twice her size,
swipes him with her dainty paw,
headlocks him into submission,
then leisurely washes his face.

Take note, I say to my teenaged sons.

Dianne Hicks Morrow

Thirteen

Nearly six feet tall, totally cool:
shock of dark hair flopped over forehead,
styling gel firmly in control,
designer jeans casually topped by
Red Eraser shirt, sleeves rolled
just so.

Mirror-approved for departure
he steps into his hundred dollar
size twelve sneakers. Big-man
hands reach to tie laces
the bunny-ear way he learned
when he was three.

Plain to Be Seen

No girls have been seduced here.
Bathtub too grotty. Wall-to-wall
never vacuumed. Bedroom floor
a crazy quilt of dirty clothes.
Brief consolation to a nosy mother
on her first visit to her son's first apartment.
Maxim on the coffee table, a new mag to her.
Inside she reads, Ten Things Women Rate You On.
Will the sight of your pad turn her off
as soon as you open the door?
A clean bathroom's not enough for the 90s woman.
Impress her with fluffy white towels, crystal
wine goblets, and a plant or two to show
you can keep something alive.

Dianne Hicks Morrow

Hormonal

Teenage rage broke the throttle.
Now only a wide screwdriver head
pushed hard and just so
forces this damn machine to life.
Menopausal rage resents
the need for a strong man.
I yank and yank on the ripcord,
face reddening, arms whining.
Mother-son mechanics
erupt in my scream.

All I want is the soothing
drone of motor,
guaranteed sweat,
heart pounding, legs marching
round and round this country lawn.
Two hours for my own thoughts
whatever they are.

Next time I see him, I tell my son
we have something in common.

Familiars

Alone I Drive

My swimming friend's
a writer who lives alone.

At a golf fundraiser she is
poet laureate; I chair
the worthy cause.
We're both outsiders to the games
of well-tended middle-aged men
who like to leer at women
who've never tended them.

Time to go. She says,
"Want to have a swim?"
I say, "Let's go to my house first
to pick up the kids."
Her smile fades.
"Oh I don't think there's time."
We hug goodbye.

Alone I drive along the shore:
blue sky meets spring green.
Beyond a sandstone cliff,
a lone woman in a black swimsuit
strides into the cold sea.

I take my foot off the gas,
then push down hard.

54

Escapades

I can tell you that
I've figured out how to leave the dickweed I married,
get a full-time job, support myself and the kids,
move to a housing co-op with other single moms
and a shared playground.
You know
I'm just plotting an escape
I don't really want to act on.

And you can tell me that
you're spending the day up a tree
hiding from the high testosterone levels
of your own particular monkey.
I know
you'll come down in time
to celebrate your twenty-fifth anniversary
next week.

We stay on stand-by for each other,
just in case.

Dianne Hicks Morrow

Edith Lulu (1883–1973)

Less than three pounds,
swaddled in a shoe box
behind the wood stove,
you lived,
your head smaller
than a teacup,
your arms so thin
they say your mother's
wedding ring went
all the way
to your shoulder.

Just four-feet-eleven, grown,
who'd have thought you
would give birth ten times?
Graydon, Henrietta,
Eileen, Guy, Lorne,
Iris, Leah, Talmage,
Linden, and Eric.

Ten babies born
on the old homestead,
in the stove-warmed bedroom
off the kitchen.
Seven reminisce
today at Iris' eightieth
birthday party.
You saw ninety.
They wonder if they will
as they stoke the legend
of your miraculous
survival.

Aunt Henrietta

1. Ninety-First

Above your bed you
and your older brother stare
from behind bevelled glass.
His solemn blue eyes, jug ears,
wavy hair slicked into place.
Your floppy hair ribbon and wide-open smile,
unafraid of the strange eye
peering at you from its black tent.
You're three, he's five.
Eight other brothers and sisters to come
will never be framed so elegantly.

Under the oval frame three siblings chat.
The only one who'll remember this visit
is the brother who drove six hours
to get here for your ninety-first birthday.
When your stroked voice slurs,
"I s'pose you'll have a big Christmas dinner,"
he cups his ear. "Christmas winner?
Did you win something?"
Your younger sister says, "Henrietta
and I still play a mean game of Scrabble,"
but she won't know an hour
from now that she and her brother were here.

57

2. It's Time

Your beak
and glittering eyes
dart from side to side.
From the birdcage
of your hospital bed
you discern three men
with haloes backlit
by the window: younger brothers
cluck their concern but can't
make out stroke-muffled words.
Your claws try to clutch ice cream
only you can see.

I wonder if you weigh your age.
Revered oldest sister, second
mother to nine siblings.
Had no children of your own.
My father wanted to name me
Henrietta Pamelia, after you.
My mother spared me
Henny Penny for short.

Dad refuses to go in my car
on the long drive to see you.
Says, "I keep this old car
in perfect shape. As long as I
can drive, I'm going to."

You fought your age too,
drove as long as you could.
Now it's time
to fly,
if only you could.

Slide Show

This is my family home on Waterloo Row.
See how the lace-curtain sun
patterns the grand staircase.
My painting prof said I'd never be good—
I grew up too rich to suffer.

I learned from the next painting that
you don't have to do everything right,
just one thing—the thing that saves it:
the long Saran Wrap folds
in the shadow of this trout.

I hope no one points out
to the young couple who
bought this barbecue scene
how like a crematorium it is.
They love to cook out.

Here is my eldest in her wedding
dress. Daughters can break
your heart. I like this painting better—
the same dress hanging
limp on the clothesline.

This is the most vicious painting I ever
did of Helen, the nude
who posed for Christopher over the years.
I always paint from photos—she's
looking at my husband here, not me.

At last I've suffered
enough to paint ugly:
this stripped moose
carcass hung to cure.

Dianne Hicks Morrow

Archaeological

"With five babies in seven years
I thought I'd never dig again."
At a ho-hum Christmas party
she holds court, sweeps
wispy white hair back
from her high forehead
with gnarled hands,
her regal back model-straight.
Aegean-blue eyes hold us floating
at their whim,
stormy seas imminent.
She throws a don't-you-dare
look to her husband. For once
this is going to be her story.

"One died of cancer at four.
I wanted to die too.
Friends with only two children
offered to take ours that summer.
Said they wanted to experience
a big family, have brothers for their girls."
Her yellowed-tooth smile dazzles.
"So I got to Greece again.
I've gone back now
for twenty-seven summers.
My glass is empty.
Who's pouring?"

Sausaged

I remember the big deal
over his sausages:
cooked just so,
evenly browned
all the way round,
crisp but never burnt,
his wife and kids heaping frantic praise,
"My, these taste soooo good.
Doesn't Dad cook the best sausages?"

Of course any man
could cook perfect
sausages with his
wife making
the rest of the meal.

I remember
my ten-year-old friend
and nine-year-old me
giggling in bed
ready for a repeat
of her mother's refrain,
"If you two don't
stop giggling and go
to sleep, I'm going
to separate you."

Dianne Hicks Morrow

But we get
her father flinging
open the bedroom
door, the light from
the hallway making
deep caves of his small
eyes, as he spits out the words,
"See this leather belt?
Shut up or I'll let you have it!"

One look at my friend's face,
fear-stained, shows me
why his sausages are such a big deal.

All Those Years

The luncheon speaker has finished,
thirty women are ready to leave.
Two eighty-year-olds linger,
sizing each other up.
I rush over and ask the petite one,
elegant in her clan tartan suit,
"Hazel, you know Gerda, don't you?"
Gerda's deep voice answers,
a what-the-hell expression on her face,
as she buttons up her plaid logger shirt,
"Yes, indeed, she knows me.
Many say my husband, long deceased,
married me on the rebound from Hazel."
Hazel fingers her Scottish thistle pin,
darts Gerda a nervous look,
"It's true I loved your Robert,
but my parents wouldn't let me marry him!"
"No wonder. He didn't have a cent to his name!"
"And he became a Communist!"
"Nope, I was the Communist, not Robert. But you
were too rich for him. He couldn't
even get a membership at your tennis club."

Gerda looks at me,
"You know, I always envied Hazel and wondered
if Robert ever got over her."
"But think how I envied you. You had him!"
"Dunno if he was that great a catch!"

Dianne Hicks Morrow

Uproarious laughter, then some tears.
"Think of all those years we avoided each other
at Peace Committee meetings," says Hazel,
teetering in her high heels.
Rubber-booted Gerda offers Hazel
her arm as they walk out.

64

Polio Kick

In the Pool

We swim leisurely lengths.
I ask my mother, "Did Dad flood
our backyard to make the rink
when I was little or did God?"
All that work for a kid who'd never
be able to skate alone.

"You're not going to write another poem
about polio, are you? One was all right,
but you don't want anyone to think you're fixated."

Breath stops. Heart pounds.
We keep swimming. At last I say,
"I don't care what anyone thinks."

After forty-seven years
holding my breath, it's
time.

I am on a polio kick.

Mother Script

Think how lucky you are to be alive.
No iron lung for you.
If they'd known it was polio
they'd have drained fluid off your spine
so you'd have two good feet and legs.
Instead the doctor treated you for fever at home,
the first time you were ever sick.
This is the picture of you that day.
I sent the door-to-door photographer away,
then called him back in case you were so sick you died.

> *In the photo I look fevered, but fat*
> *and strong, just seven months old*
> *in the flowered wing chair.*

I know I sterilized everything.
I was so worried because of my sight.
The doctor said I may have had things *too* clean.
When I was pregnant I prayed,
Please God, let her have her father's good brown eyes.
The first thing I asked the nurse was
What colour are her eyes?
I didn't know how few babies
are born with brown ones.
You were one.

Dianne Hicks Morrow

Mirror

"You mean if I have surgery my skinny
leg will look like my big one, Mommy?"

"Well, no, dear. You'll be able to walk better."

Puzzled, I look in her full-length
mirror and watch as she tells me to
lift up my right foot. For the first time
I see how it drops, how I have to lift my
knee too high to keep from stubbing my toe.

I've seen people who walked like that.
I didn't know I was one of them.

Under the Knife

I'm eight years old,
too young to know
the flickering fire
in the corner
of my drugged eye
is an EXIT sign,
a door I can't walk to,
or that the elephant
crushing my foot
is the pain
of truncated tendons.

Thirteen now,
I am afraid this night
before surgery,
still hugging
the stuffed fawn
Mom has left.
Tears darken his white tail.
The apple juice I spill
on his hind leg looks like
pee. I grin, forget my fear
of freshly fused bone.

Dianne Hicks Morrow

Wheelchair Races

Long before Sports
for the Disabled
we whoop warning
to the nurses,
blast-off
from the ramp,
race all the way
to the end
of the endless
corridor.
Torn between
duty and joy
they cheer us on.

Confirmation

Bishop's blessing,
my Mother's white
wedding dress, cut off
to show my brace-free leg
and white bucks. No
hated oxfords for
this special day
when God
confirms I am.

Dianne Hicks Morrow

Prosthesis

She stands on her bed, eyes in the mirror
holding the fabric just so,
eight inches above the ankles
where an overmuscled leg
and a withered one almost match.
She dreams of the day she'll be old enough
to wear her skirt that long,
born too early for the bluejean craze
that would make her look like everyone else.

When miniskirts become the fad
she gets a zip-on mould, skin-toned.
Covered by tights, it looks just like her big leg.
The spongy form gives her a reprieve
from *the look*,
the one guys give her
the first time they notice
and turn off.

72

Ass

We're in the line-up for our shots.
The nurse preps my arm and says,
"What soft, smooth skin."
I blush as she winks
at the cute guy
behind me.

I'd had a crush on him until
he confessed he always thought
I was great but couldn't ask me out
because of my "(uh) limp, I know it isn't right,
but I just can't handle (uh), you know,
deformity."

Later I overhear him say
to his gorgeous girlfriend,
who thinks she is knock-kneed,
"Don't worry about your legs.
They just go up and make
an ass of themselves."

73

Impostures

"Focus your eyes on a point in front of you.
Now shift all your weight onto your right foot.
Slowly make circles in the air with your left leg
without losing your balance."

Easy for her to say
with her straight strong legs.
I touch my right hand to the column
I've chosen to be near
in this charming library ashram.
When will it be over? Time
for the other side, my good left foot
and leg, overmuscled to make up for
polio-thinned right.
I envy other legs
—fat ones, skinny ones, bowed ones—
they match.

Later I hear
a radio interviewer say
she knows how it feels to
protect a broken foot.
It's on her mind every
moment of every day.
But hers can heal.
My traitor ankle can turn,
drop me without warning,
force me to admit
I am unbalanced.

Reachers

In our backyard rink I skate with a chair,
feel safe enough to let go: fall,
black out, see stars.
Sonja Henie overcame her polio,
became a famous figure skater.
I love whirling in circles,
the whoosh of wind in my ears,
weight on my good leg, unable to lap.
Lacking balance, I cannot skate alone.

My parents are poetry on ice:
Mom in her long-bladed reachers,
Dad in his old hockey skates.
Others stop to watch them glide,
cover the rink in three strokes,
she on his arm, the ideal couple.
Mom's balance is perfect, but
lacking sight, she cannot skate alone.

Sparkling gem of memory:
miles of crystal ice on Spruce Lake,
my parents and I, joyful trio.
Dad in the middle, keeping me balanced,
being Mom's eyes. When my
feet tire, my parents skate off.
I remember Sonja, and whirl,
collapse on snow at the edge.
My parents shrink to icons.

Dianne Hicks Morrow

I soon quit skating,
couldn't stand the gap between
dream and reality. Mom and Dad
kept it up until a few years ago.
He was afraid of breaking bones.
She wonders if stopping
was the right thing.
So do I.

Home

Poplar leaf rustle

kept me awake
living alone
in my first garret,
yellow lichen trunks
bright against the grey harbour
in drab November.
When the muttering leaves
let go,
I wrote poetry there.

Now I live in the country.
Balm of Gilead poplars
whisper behind this house,
replace twenty years of kidnoise.
Outside the upstairs window
I see crooked trunks
growing their first
yellow lichens,
leaves ready
to let go.

78

telescoping
time
around
rustle
poplar
leaves

Hay Fever

She'd like to leap
into the void
but she's afraid,
recalls other leaps—
the drop from the hayloft window
into prickly pillows,
golden motes,
eyes streaming hay histamines.
She felt her way up the ladder
stumbled over slippery bales
to the top once more,
then leapt into
the scream
triumphant.
Oh, to be that kid again,
bringing on hay fever.

Dianne Hicks Morrow

Old House

When we first moved
into this old house
I'd imagine wood stove
flames reaching the sky
every time I'd round the curve
home, too late to save anything.
Or I'd feel the stove's cast iron
weight pulling me through
the spongy floor into
a basement inferno.
Now crooked windows tell me
carpenter ants will win.
Salamanders still hide in the damp
cellar, peering from prehistory.
My slow-motion house sinks
into its sandstone foundation
one memory at a time.

The Devil Sends

The truck dumps topsoil on the grass
at the end of our long clay lane,
the place the west wind burns by August.
Barefoot I jump in the loamy earth,
decide to make a rock garden.
My husband wheelbarrows huge
foundation stones to circle the base.
Our sons bring bricks from the torn-down
chimney. One builds steps to the top for fun
facing north, away from the house.
I ask him to make more on the south side
to see from the kitchen window.
Don't know until too late
I've turned play into work.

Granddad gives a wrought iron sundial for the top.
"Gonna be some job to keep the weeds out of this."
For the first years we call it the Shinto
shrine. Nasturtiums border brick stairs.
Dainty carpathian harebells thrive
a while. Hardy rock garden perennials grow
then die. Even sturdy sedum. The herb
quadrant goes wild. Dill disappears.
God steps in, gives wild strawberries.
Next, buttercups, Queen Anne's
lace, asters, and goldenrod.
Then the Devil sends the sod
that finally takes over.
Our sons have left home.
Only the forget-me-nots bloom now.

gardener's
(knowledge)
wisdom 81

Dianne Hicks Morrow

Picture this:

a big-boned, ample-girthed,
middle-aged couple
cutting, piecing, gluing
heavy vinyl wallpaper,
bending behind the toilet,
fitting under the sink
sliding paper behind the pipes
on a polygon floor so small
the longest side can't hold
a normal-sized bathtub,
and the shower nozzle
aims at the lint in the bellybutton
of anyone over five-foot-ten.

I lie back in my bath and
admire the new Santa Fe paper,
pattern perfectly matched,
its cool teal a counterpoint
to the ceramic tiles' warm sandstone,
a colour common to The Island and the mesa.

The first time I stripped
paper from the gable slope
it came off in thumb-sized pieces
no matter how much I wetted it.
I banged my forehead on that slope
in frustration.
I feared the tiles I glued
above the tub would let go and crash
on a bubble bather's head.
Such elegant tiles
called for classy wallpaper.
We failed to hang it
harmoniously—he new
to papering, I too bossy.

But the grey pussy willows
on ochre linen backing
did not come unglued
until recently.

This time he picks out the paper,
helps me predict where
the seams will come
and how to piece the strips.
We apply the wide Navajo border
that binds and blends the colours
this morning,
our twenty-third anniversary.

Dianne Hicks Morrow

That Won't Let Go

Time to take the Sunday River
decal off the door.
We never did get there.
Now the kids can go
on their own
if they want.

We four did a lot of trips.
Photo albums document
adventures winter and summer.
It's the ones we didn't take
I remember most.

The chalet on the ski hill,
the boys schussing by the picture window,
my feet up near the fireplace
after a bracing cross-country ski
with you through beeches
still burnished by leaves
that won't let go.

84

Acknowledgements

The long journey that led to the creation of this book had many guides along the way, who offered what I needed at the time, whether I knew it or not. Some of those guides, to whom I give grateful thanks, are Fred Cogswell, the first poet I ever met and my favourite professor at UNB; Anne McCallum, editor of *Common Ground*, who first published my writing; Deirdre Kessler, whose workshop advice "to write about what haunts you" allowed me to look at the unspoken theme of disability in my family; June Blair, who said, "I don't think you want to do a Master's Degree—I think you want to write and Bob will work with you," and her partner Bob Simmons, who helped me shape my first short story and pointed me toward poetry; Frank Ledwell, who taught my first university creative writing course and gave me confidence in my own voice; Richard Lemm, who helped me take more risks; Janice Kulyk Keefer, who told me to "fall forward into the dark" as Robert Frost said, not knowing it was Frost's work that first drew me to poetry; Ladeez Ox writing group members, Laurie Brinklow, Elaine Hammond, and Eliza Jane Wilson, without whose encouragement and prodding I'd have never entered a poetry contest or had a manuscript.

My heartfelt gratitude to the P.E.I. Writers' Guild for fostering new writers; the P.E.I. Council of the Arts for a grant that allowed me some time to develop this manuscript; Acorn Press Publisher Laurie Brinklow, whose belief in Prince Edward Island writing leads her to take shocking financial risks for art; and to editor Jane Ledwell (Frank's eldest), whose keen eye, heart, and mind shaped the book.

A huge thank you to my husband Andrew and sons Michael and Jacob, who make me laugh when I take things too seriously and give me the kind of support I need, whether I know it or not.

About the author

Dianne Hicks Morrow draws on rich connections both to Atlantic Canada's islands and its mainland. She was conceived in Newfoundland, married a Prince Edward Islander, and gave birth to two Islanders. She knows she may never fully qualify as an Islander but would not, in any case, trade in her mainland roots and relations. She was born and raised in Saint John, New Brunswick, graduated from UNB in Fredericton, and taught high school in Vancouver before moving back east to the farmhouse she shares with her husband Andrew on Prince Edward Island's North Shore. Her love of rivers and oceans flows through her poems.

Her award-winning poems have appeared in journals across Canada, including *The Abegweit Review, Common Ground, Contemporary Verse 2, Pottersfield Portfolio,* and *The Windsor Review,* as well as in *A Woman's Almanac: Voices from Atlantic Canada* (1995), *Enchanted Companions: Stories of Dolls in Our Lives* (Storyweaver, 2001), and *Landmarks: An Anthology of New Atlantic Canadian Poetry of the Land* (The Acorn Press, 2001), and on CBC Radio's Island Morning, Main Street, Information Morning for the Maritimes, and The Live Poets Society. Her poetry has won prizes in the Prince Edward Island Literary Awards and the Atlantic Writing Competition.